Île de Ré travel guide

The Ultimate Guide to Île de Ré: Your Passport to Paradise

Janice Hamilton

Copyright ©2023 by [Name], All Rights Reserved.

This travel guide book is protected by copyright law and international copyright treaties. No part of this travel guide book may be reproduced, stored in a retrieval system, or transmitted in any form or by any means, electronic, mechanical, photocopying, recording, scanning, or otherwise, without the prior written permission of the copyright owner.

Table of Contents

1. Introduction to Île de Ré
- Discovering the Gem of the Atlantic Coast
- Unique Charm of Île de Ré
- Practical Information for Travelers

2. Planning Your Trip
- Best Time to Visit Île de Ré
- How to Get to Île de Ré
- Visa and Travel Requirements
- Currency, Language, and Local Etiquette

3. Accommodations
- Luxury Resorts and Boutique Hotels
- Charming Bed and Breakfasts
- Budget-Friendly Options
- Camping on Île de Ré

4. Exploring the Island
- Overview of Île de Ré's Geography
- Must-Visit Villages and Towns

- Getting Around: Bicycles, Cars, and Public Transportation
- Insider Tips for Navigating the Island

5. Beaches of Île de Ré

- Sun, Sand, and Surf: An Overview
- Best Beaches for Swimming
- Watersports and Activities
- Hidden Beach Gems

6. Culture and History

- The Rich Heritage of Île de Ré
- Museums, Art Galleries, and Exhibitions
- Festivals and Events
- Local Cuisine and Culinary Traditions

7. Outdoor Adventures

- Hiking and Nature Trails
- Bird Watching in Île de Ré's Natural Reserves
- Watersports and Sailing
- Golf Courses and Tennis Courts

8. Shopping and Souvenirs
- Unique Boutiques and Markets
- Traditional Island Products
- Where to Buy Handmade Crafts
- Tax-Free Shopping Tips

9. Dining and Nightlife
- Authentic Île de Ré Cuisine
- Local Seafood Specialties
- Beachfront Dining and Romantic Eateries
- Nightclubs and Entertainment

10. Family-Friendly Activities
- Kid-Friendly Beaches and Playgrounds
- Family-Friendly Attractions
- Tips for Traveling with Children

11. Wellness and Relaxation
- Spas and Wellness Centers
- Yoga Retreats

Meditation and Mindfulness on the Island

12. Practical Tips and Safety
- Health and Safety Information
- Packing Essentials for Île de Ré
- Emergency Contacts and Services
- Sustainable Travel Practices

13. Day Trips and Excursions
- Exploring Nearby Islands
- Mainland Adventures
- Wine Tasting in the Surrounding Region
- Organized Tours and Excursions

14. Local Insights and Hidden Gems
- Off the Beaten Path Destinations
- Locals' Favorite Spots
- Insider Tips for an Authentic Experience

15. Conclusion
- Farewell to Île de Ré
- Memories to Cherish
- Planning Your Next Adventure

This travel guide provides you with all the essential information you need to explore the picturesque Île de Ré, from its stunning beaches to its rich cultural heritage.

Whether you're a solo traveler, a family seeking adventure, or a couple seeking romance, Île de Ré has something for everyone. Dive into this guide, and let your Île de Ré adventure begin!

1. Introduction to Île de Ré

- Discovering the Gem of the Atlantic Coast

Welcome to the enchanting world of Île de Ré, a hidden gem nestled off the coast of western France. This exquisite island, often referred to as the "Pearl of the Atlantic," offers a captivating blend of natural beauty, rich history, and vibrant culture.

As you embark on your journey to Île de Ré, prepare to be transported to a place where time seems to slow down, and every moment feels like a cherished memory in the making.

From the moment you step foot on this island paradise, you'll be greeted by a landscape of pristine sandy beaches, picturesque harbors, and lush salt marshes.

The island's unique geography and gentle climate make it a haven for those seeking relaxation and outdoor adventure alike.

Whether you're drawn to the soothing rhythm of the waves or the thrill of exploring nature reserves and hiking trails, Île de Ré has it all.

- Unique Charm of Île de Ré

What sets Île de Ré apart is its unspoiled, timeless charm. The island's traditional white-washed houses with their green or blue shutters, narrow winding streets, and charming villages evoke a sense of nostalgia.

As you stroll through the cobblestone lanes, you'll be captivated by the authentic atmosphere that harks back to a simpler era. The absence of high-rise buildings and commercialization preserves the island's unique character, making it a haven for those seeking authenticity.

The island's rich history is palpable in every corner. Dating back to Roman times, Île de Ré has been shaped by centuries of maritime heritage, fortified towns, and maritime trade.

The iconic St. Martin de Ré, a UNESCO World Heritage Site, stands as a testament to this history, with its impressive fortifications and picturesque harbor.

But Île de Ré is not just about history; it's also a vibrant, living community. Locals take pride in their island and its traditions, and you'll find them warmly welcoming visitors into their world.

Explore bustling markets, savor mouthwatering seafood at quaint restaurants, and engage with the island's cultural events to get a taste of its authentic spirit.

- Practical Information for Travelers

Before you embark on your Île de Ré adventure, it's essential to arm yourself with practical information to ensure a smooth and enjoyable experience. This section of the guide will provide you with valuable insights into the island's logistics, ensuring you're well-prepared for your journey.

You'll learn about the best times to visit Île de Ré, taking into account weather conditions and local events. We'll guide you through the various transportation options available to reach the island, including details on ferry services and the nearby La Rochelle airport.

Additionally, we'll provide essential information regarding visa requirements, currency exchange, language tips, and local etiquette, ensuring you're ready to immerse yourself in the island's culture with confidence.

As you turn the page, you'll find yourself on the threshold of an extraordinary adventure.

Welcome to Île de Ré, where beauty, history, and culture await your exploration. Get ready to uncover the treasures of this Atlantic Coast gem, one page at a time.

2. Planning Your Trip

- Best Time to Visit Île de Ré

Choosing the perfect time to visit Île de Ré is crucial to ensure you experience the island's beauty and activities to the fullest. The island's climate, landscapes, and cultural events vary with the seasons, so let's explore the best times to plan your trip.

Spring (March to May): Spring is a fantastic time to visit Île de Ré. The weather begins to warm up, and the island bursts into color as flowers bloom. You'll enjoy quieter beaches and a more relaxed atmosphere, making it an ideal period for those seeking tranquility and outdoor adventures like cycling and hiking.

Summer (June to August): This is the high season when Île de Ré comes alive with tourists and locals alike. The weather is warm and sunny, perfect for beach lovers and water sports enthusiasts. The island hosts various festivals and events during this time, offering a glimpse into its vibrant culture.

Autumn (September to November): If you prefer milder temperatures and fewer crowds, consider visiting in the fall. The island retains its natural beauty, and you can still enjoy outdoor activities. September is particularly pleasant, with warm waters for swimming.

Winter (December to February): While the island is quieter during the winter months, it has its unique charm. The peaceful atmosphere and crisp air provide an excellent backdrop for exploring historical sites and enjoying cozy evenings by the fireplace. Keep in mind that some businesses may have limited hours or be closed during this season.

- How to Get to Île de Ré

Getting to Île de Ré is an adventure in itself, and the journey adds to the island's allure. Here are the primary ways to reach this idyllic destination:

By Car: If you're driving from mainland France, you can access Île de Ré via the

3-kilometer-long toll bridge, Pont de Ré, which connects it to La Rochelle. This is the most common method for travelers with their vehicles.

By Train: Take a train to La Rochelle's train station, Gare de La Rochelle, and from there, you can hop on a bus or hire a taxi to reach the island. The scenic train ride along the Atlantic coast is a delightful experience.

By Air: Fly into La Rochelle Airport (La Rochelle-Île de Ré Airport) if you prefer air travel. The airport is well-connected to major French cities and international destinations. From the airport, you can reach Île de Ré via taxi or a shuttle service.

- Visa and Travel Requirements

Traveling to Île de Ré is relatively straightforward for most international visitors due to its location within France's Schengen Area. However, it's essential to ensure you meet the necessary visa and travel requirements before your trip. Here's a brief overview:

Schengen Visa: If you're from a country outside the Schengen Area, make sure you have the appropriate Schengen visa for your planned stay duration. Check with the French embassy or consulate in your home country for specific requirements.

Passport: Ensure that your passport is valid for at least six months beyond your planned departure date from Île de Ré.

Travel Insurance: Consider purchasing travel insurance that covers unexpected events, including medical emergencies, trip cancellations, and lost luggage.

Currency, Language, and Local Etiquette

Understanding the local currency, language, and etiquette will help you navigate Île de Ré with ease and show respect to the island's culture and people.

Currency: The official currency of Île de Ré, as part of France, is the Euro (EUR). Credit and debit cards are widely accepted, but it's a good idea to carry some cash for small purchases and places that may not accept cards.

Language: French is the primary language spoken on Île de Ré, and while many locals may understand some English, it's helpful to learn a few basic French phrases. The effort to speak the local language is often appreciated by residents.

Local Etiquette: Islanders are known for their warm hospitality and politeness. When greeting someone, a simple "Bonjour" (good morning) or "Bonsoir" (good evening) goes a long way. Tipping is customary in restaurants, and it's polite to leave a small tip for good service.

As you embark on planning your trip to Île de Ré, consider these essential factors to ensure a smooth and enjoyable adventure on this captivating island. Whether you're a nature enthusiast, a history buff, or simply seeking relaxation, Île de Ré has something extraordinary to offer.

3. Accommodations

One of the key elements in planning a memorable stay on Île de Ré is choosing the right accommodation. The island offers a diverse range of lodging options to cater to different tastes and budgets. Whether you prefer the lap of luxury, the charm of a cozy bed and breakfast, the practicality of budget-friendly lodging, or the adventure of camping, Île de Ré has you covered.

- Luxury Resorts and Boutique Hotels

If your idea of a perfect vacation involves pampering, opulence, and the finest amenities, then Île de Ré's luxury resorts and boutique hotels will not disappoint. These establishments are designed to provide an indulgent and unforgettable experience.

Luxury Resorts: Choose from a selection of renowned luxury resorts, often located near the island's stunning beaches. These resorts offer spacious rooms, world-class dining, spa facilities, and a range of activities such as golf, tennis, and water sports. Revel in the breathtaking sea views and personalized service that these resorts are known for.

Boutique Hotels: For a more intimate and unique experience, consider staying at one of the island's boutique hotels. These charming properties blend modern comforts with the island's traditional aesthetics. You'll find individually decorated rooms, personalized service, and a cozy atmosphere that ensures a memorable stay.

- Charming Bed and Breakfasts

For travelers seeking a more personal and homey atmosphere, the bed and breakfasts on Île de Ré are an excellent choice. These charming accommodations are often run by friendly locals who are passionate about sharing the island's culture with their guests.

Warm Hospitality: Bed and breakfast hosts are known for their warm hospitality. Wake up to a homemade breakfast featuring local ingredients and receive personalized recommendations for exploring the island.

Authentic Ambiance: The décor of these establishments often reflects the island's maritime heritage and traditional architecture. Expect comfortable rooms with unique touches that create a cozy and welcoming ambiance.

- Budget-Friendly Options

Travelers on a budget will find several cost-effective accommodations on Île de Ré. These options allow you to experience the island's beauty without breaking the bank.

Camping: Camping is a budget-friendly way to enjoy Île de Ré's natural beauty up close. There are several well-equipped campgrounds across the island, offering facilities like showers, toilets, and even on-site stores. Pitch your tent or rent a caravan or mobile home for a memorable outdoor experience.

Hostels and Guesthouses: Some hostels and guesthouses provide affordable lodging options, particularly for solo travelers or those on a tight budget. While they may offer fewer amenities than luxury resorts, these accommodations still provide a comfortable and convenient place to stay.

- Camping on Île de Ré

Camping enthusiasts and nature lovers will find Île de Ré to be a paradise for outdoor adventures. Camping on the island is an exciting way to connect with its natural beauty and experience a sense of freedom.

Scenic Campgrounds: Île de Ré boasts picturesque campgrounds, often situated near the coastline or within nature reserves. Wake up to the sound of the waves or the chirping of birds, and enjoy stunning sunsets from your campsite.

Activities: Camping on Île de Ré offers an array of outdoor activities, from beachcombing and swimming to hiking and birdwatching. Many campgrounds organize nature-oriented programs and activities for guests of all ages.

Facilities: Campgrounds on the island typically offer essential amenities such as showers, toilets, laundry facilities, and communal cooking areas. Some may also have on-site restaurants or cafes where you can savor local cuisine.

As you plan your visit to Île de Ré, consider your preferences and budget to choose the accommodation that best suits your needs. Whether you opt for luxury, embrace the charm of a bed and breakfast, prioritize budget-conscious options, or embrace the great outdoors through camping, your choice of lodging will play a significant role in shaping your Île de Ré experience.

4. Exploring the Island

Overview of Île de Ré's Geography

Before embarking on your exploration of Île de Ré, it's essential to acquaint yourself with the island's unique geography. Île de Ré, located off the Atlantic coast of France, is a slender, elongated island measuring about 30 kilometers in length and just 5 kilometers at its widest point. This distinctive shape means that, no matter where you are on the island, you're never far from the coast.

Coastline: The island is blessed with approximately 100 kilometers of coastline, characterized by pristine sandy beaches, dunes, and dramatic cliffs. The varied coastline offers diverse experiences, from serene sunbathing spots to dynamic surfing beaches.

Salt Marshes: One of the island's defining features is its extensive salt marshes. These marshes are not only ecologically significant but also create a unique landscape that is both picturesque and ecologically important. You can explore them on guided tours and learn about the traditional salt production methods still in use today.

Villages and Towns: The island is dotted with charming villages and towns, each with its own character and history. These settlements often feature narrow cobblestone streets, white-washed houses adorned with colorful shutters, and bustling markets. The island's heart is St. Martin de Ré, a UNESCO World Heritage Site, known for its historical fortifications and vibrant harbor.

- Must-Visit Villages and Towns

Exploring the villages and towns of Île de Ré is like stepping back in time to a simpler, more idyllic era. Here are some must-visit locations that will capture your heart:

St. Martin de Ré: The island's capital, St. Martin de Ré, is a gem of a town with its fortifications, charming streets, and lively harbor. Explore the historic citadel, visit the

Vauban fortifications, and enjoy fresh seafood at waterfront restaurants.

La Flotte: This picturesque village is known for its flower-lined streets, bustling market square, and beautiful harbor. It's an excellent place to take a leisurely stroll and admire traditional architecture.

Ars-en-Ré: Located at the western tip of the island, Ars-en-Ré is famous for its black-and-white striped church tower. The town has a unique maritime atmosphere and is an ideal spot to watch sunsets.

Le Bois-Plage-en-Ré: With its long sandy beach, vibrant market, and charming village center, Le Bois-Plage-en-Ré is a popular destination for beachgoers and shoppers alike.

Getting Around: Bicycles, Cars, and Public Transportation

Navigating Île de Ré is a delightful experience, thanks to its well-maintained infrastructure and dedication to sustainable transportation. Here's how to get around the island:

Bicycles: Île de Ré is renowned for its extensive network of cycling paths that crisscross the island. Rent a bicycle to explore the picturesque villages, beaches, and natural reserves at your own pace. Biking is not only eco-friendly but also allows you to immerse yourself in the island's beauty.

Cars: While cars are allowed on the island, it's worth noting that traffic can be congested during peak tourist season. Nevertheless, having a car can be convenient, especially if you plan to explore more remote areas or have mobility concerns.

Public Transportation: Île de Ré has a reliable and efficient bus network that connects its towns and villages. Additionally, there's a small train that runs between St. Martin de Ré and La Rochelle, providing an alternative to driving.

- Insider Tips for Navigating the Island

To make the most of your visit to Île de Ré, here are some insider tips for navigating the island like a seasoned traveler:

Explore by Bicycle: Consider renting a bicycle during your stay. It's the preferred mode of transportation for many visitors and allows you to access even the most secluded spots with ease.

Visit Early or Late: To avoid crowds and make the most of popular destinations like St.

Martin de Ré and the beaches, plan to visit early in the morning or later in the afternoon.

Try Local Cuisine: Don't miss out on trying local specialties such as seafood, oysters, and salted caramel treats. The island's culinary scene is a highlight of any visit.

Respect Nature: Île de Ré is home to a delicate ecosystem, so be mindful of the environment. Stay on designated paths, avoid disturbing wildlife, and pick up after yourself.

Plan for Parking: If you're driving, be prepared for limited parking in popular areas, especially during peak season. Consider using public transportation or cycling for short trips.

Familiarize with Tides: Keep an eye on tide schedules if you plan water-based activities.

Some beaches may become inaccessible during high tide.

As you embark on your adventure on Île de Ré, armed with knowledge about its geography, must-visit destinations, transportation options, and insider tips, you're sure to have an unforgettable experience exploring this captivating island. Whether you're drawn to its history, natural beauty, or vibrant culture, Île de Ré has something extraordinary to offer every traveler.

5. Beaches of Île de Ré

- Sun, Sand, and Surf: An Overview

Île de Ré is renowned for its sun-kissed beaches that stretch along its coastline, offering visitors a paradise for relaxation and recreation. With over 100 kilometers of shoreline, you'll find a beach for every preference, from family-friendly spots to hidden coves where you can escape the crowds.

The island's beaches are characterized by fine golden sand, dunes adorned with wildflowers, and crystal-clear waters. Whether you're looking to bask in the sun, swim in the Atlantic Ocean, or engage in water sports, the beaches of Île de Ré provide a serene backdrop for your coastal adventures.

- Best Beaches for Swimming

Swimming is one of the most popular activities on Île de Ré, thanks to its calm and relatively warm waters. Here are some of the best beaches for taking a dip:

Le Bois-Plage-en-Ré Beach: Located on the southern coast, this expansive beach is ideal for swimming and sunbathing. It's known for its gentle waves and shallow waters, making it a great choice for families with children.

La Couarde-sur-Mer Beach: Another family-friendly option, this beach boasts a wide sandy shore and safe swimming conditions. The nearby town offers restaurants and ice cream shops for a convenient seaside meal.

Rivedoux-Plage Beach: Close to the bridge connecting Île de Ré to the mainland, this beach is easily accessible and a favorite among locals. Its calm waters are perfect for swimming, and you can also try windsurfing or kiteboarding here.

Plage de Trousse-Chemise: Nestled on the island's western coast, this beach is surrounded by pine forests and dunes, providing a tranquil atmosphere. It's a great spot for a relaxing swim and a leisurely walk along the shoreline.

- Watersports and Activities

For those seeking a bit more excitement, Île de Ré offers a variety of water sports and activities to keep you entertained:

Windsurfing and Kiteboarding: The island's favorable winds and shallow waters make it an excellent destination for windsurfing and kiteboarding. Several rental shops and schools offer equipment and lessons for both beginners and experienced riders.

Sailing: The island's numerous marinas and sailing schools cater to sailing enthusiasts. Whether you're a seasoned sailor or a novice looking for a guided excursion, you'll find opportunities to explore the waters surrounding Île de Ré.

Surfing: The Atlantic coast of Île de Ré has some great surf spots, with waves suitable for both beginners and advanced surfers. Surf schools and equipment rental shops are available to help you catch the perfect wave.

Stand-Up Paddleboarding (SUP): Calm waters and scenic surroundings make Île de Ré an ideal place for stand-up paddleboarding. Paddle through salt marshes, along the coastline, or explore hidden coves.

- Hidden Beach Gems

While the island has its well-known beaches, there are also hidden gems waiting to be discovered:

Plage des Gollandières: Tucked away near St. Clément des Baleines, this secluded beach is surrounded by dunes and offers a tranquil escape from the crowds.

Anse du Martray: Located on the northern tip of the island, this beach is known for its unique shellfish and driftwood deposits. It's a serene and lesser-visited spot for beachcombing and relaxation.

Plage de la Conche des Baleines: This expansive stretch of sandy beach on the western coast offers breathtaking sunsets and ample space to find a quiet spot for yourself.

Plage des Prises: Found near La Couarde-sur-Mer, this picturesque beach features a combination of sand and rocks, making it perfect for exploring tide pools and watching the sunset.

Whether you're looking for a tranquil place to sunbathe, a family-friendly swimming spot, exhilarating water sports, or hidden gems off the beaten path, Île de Ré's beaches offer an array of coastal experiences for every traveler. So, pack your swimsuit and sunblock, and get ready to soak up the island's sun, sand, and surf.

6. Culture and History

The Rich Heritage of Île de Ré

Île de Ré boasts a captivating blend of history and culture that has been shaped by centuries of maritime heritage, trade, and strategic significance. As you explore the island, you'll discover its rich heritage and deep-rooted traditions that continue to influence its way of life.

Maritime Heritage: The island's history is deeply intertwined with the sea. Its strategic location along the Atlantic coast led to the construction of fortifications such as those in St. Martin de Ré, which played a crucial role in defending France. Fishing, salt production, and maritime trade have been integral to the island's economy and identity.

Fortifications: Île de Ré is home to impressive fortifications, including the Vauban fortifications in St. Martin de Ré, which are a UNESCO World Heritage Site. These fortifications are a testament to the island's historical significance in protecting France from naval invasions.

Traditional Architecture: The island's villages and towns feature traditional white-washed houses adorned with colorful shutters. This architectural style is not only visually pleasing but also functional, helping to keep the houses cool in the summer.

- Museums, Art Galleries, and Exhibitions

To delve deeper into Île de Ré's culture and history, consider visiting its museums, art galleries, and exhibitions:

Ernest Cognacq Museum: Located in St. Martin de Ré, this museum offers a comprehensive overview of the island's history and culture. It features artifacts, paintings, and exhibits that highlight the island's maritime past and traditional way of life.

Ars-en-Ré Salt Marsh Interpretation Center: Learn about the island's salt production heritage at this interactive center. Discover the traditional methods of salt production and their ecological importance in the region.

Art Galleries: Île de Ré has a thriving artistic community, and you'll find several art galleries showcasing the work of local and visiting artists. These galleries often feature paintings, sculptures, and other forms of visual art inspired by the island's natural beauty.

Temporary Exhibitions: Keep an eye out for temporary exhibitions and cultural events happening throughout the year. These events may include art exhibitions, historical displays, and cultural festivals that provide deeper insights into the island's heritage.

- Festivals and Events

Immerse yourself in Île de Ré's vibrant culture by attending one of its festivals or events:

La Flotte en Ré Jazz au Phare: This annual jazz festival in La Flotte showcases both local and international talent. Enjoy live music against the backdrop of the iconic lighthouse.

Fête de la Mer: Celebrate the sea in true island style with the Fête de la Mer (Sea Festival). This event features maritime-themed parades, seafood tastings, and traditional music performances.

Les Nuits Musicales en Ré: This classical music festival brings world-class musicians to the island. Concerts are held in various historic venues, providing a unique cultural experience.

La Fête des Baleines: This festival in St. Clément des Baleines celebrates the annual migration of whales. Enjoy exhibitions, educational activities, and nature walks that shed light on these magnificent creatures.

- Local Cuisine and Culinary Traditions

Exploring the culture of Île de Ré is incomplete without savoring its culinary delights and traditions:

Seafood: The island's proximity to the Atlantic Ocean means that seafood takes center stage in its cuisine. Try local specialties like oysters, mussels, and freshly caught fish prepared in various delicious ways.

Salt Production: The island is known for its salt marshes, and you can taste the unique fleur de sel (flower of salt) harvested here. It's a prized ingredient used to enhance the flavors of many dishes.

Potatoes: Île de Ré is famous for its early potatoes, which are celebrated for their flavor and tenderness. Sample dishes like "la pomme de terre de l'île de Ré," which showcases the island's potato in various recipes.

Culinary Festivals: Don't miss the island's culinary festivals, such as the Fête de la Pomme de Terre (Potato Festival) and the Fête de l'Huître (Oyster Festival), where you can taste local specialties and enjoy a lively atmosphere.

Local Markets: Visit the island's bustling markets to discover fresh produce, artisanal cheeses, and handmade crafts. Engaging with local vendors and trying their products is an excellent way to connect with the island's culture.

Île de Ré's culture and history are deeply rooted in its maritime traditions, architectural heritage, and culinary excellence. By exploring its museums, attending festivals, and savoring local cuisine, you'll gain a deeper appreciation for the island's unique identity and the enduring legacy of its people.

7. Outdoor Adventures

Hiking and Nature Trails

Île de Ré's diverse landscape, which includes salt marshes, dunes, forests, and coastline, offers an array of hiking and nature trails that allow you to explore the island's natural beauty up close:

Les Marais Salants Trail: This trail takes you through the island's renowned salt marshes. Follow the footpaths that wind through the marshes, offering opportunities to observe local wildlife and learn about traditional salt production.

The Coastal Path: Stretching along the island's shoreline, the coastal path offers breathtaking views of the Atlantic Ocean. Hike along the dunes, cliffs, and sandy beaches while enjoying the fresh sea breeze and the sound of waves crashing.

The Forest of Trousse-Chemise: Located on the island's west coast, this forested area offers shaded trails that lead you through a mix of pine trees and coastal vegetation. It's an excellent place for a leisurely walk or a picnic.

Bike Trails: While primarily known for cycling, Île de Ré also features numerous bike trails that double as walking paths. Explore the island at your own pace, taking in the scenic beauty and stopping at points of interest along the way.

- Bird Watching in Île de Ré's Natural Reserves

Île de Ré is a haven for bird watchers, thanks to its natural reserves and diverse avian population:

Lilleau des Niges Nature Reserve: This reserve is a paradise for bird enthusiasts. It's home to various bird species, including herons, egrets, and migrating waders. Birdwatching hides and observation points are strategically placed throughout the reserve.

Réserve Naturelle Nationale de la Pointe d'Arçay: Located at the southern tip of the island, this reserve is known for its unique combination of sand dunes, salt marshes, and lagoons. It's an ideal spot to observe both resident and migratory birds.

Guided Birdwatching Tours: Consider joining a guided birdwatching tour led by local experts who can help you spot and identify the island's avian residents. These tours offer educational insights into the island's rich biodiversity.

- Watersports and Sailing

The island's maritime location invites a range of watersports and sailing opportunities:

Windsurfing and Kiteboarding: Take advantage of Île de Ré's favorable winds and shallow waters to indulge in windsurfing and kiteboarding. Rental shops and schools are available for all skill levels.

Sailing: Île de Ré's numerous marinas and sailing schools offer the perfect setting for sailing enthusiasts. Whether you're a seasoned sailor or a novice, you can explore the island's surrounding waters.

Surfing: The island's Atlantic coast provides great surfing conditions, with waves suitable for both beginners and advanced surfers. Surf schools and rental shops offer equipment and lessons.

Stand-Up Paddleboarding (SUP): Paddleboarding is a popular activity on the island. Calm waters and picturesque surroundings make Île de Ré an ideal place for SUP adventures.

- Golf Courses and Tennis Courts

For those who enjoy sports on land, Île de Ré offers golf courses and tennis courts amid its natural beauty:

Golf de Trousse-Chemise: This 9-hole golf course near Les Portes-en-Ré offers stunning views of the ocean and the surrounding natural landscape. Golfers of all levels can enjoy a round in this picturesque setting.

Tennis Courts: Many villages and resorts on Île de Ré have tennis courts available for visitors. Whether you're a casual player or a tennis enthusiast, you can enjoy a game while soaking up the island's atmosphere.

Golf and Tennis Clubs: Consider taking lessons or participating in tournaments at golf and tennis clubs on the island. These clubs offer a chance to improve your skills and connect with fellow enthusiasts.

Île de Ré's outdoor adventures cater to a wide range of interests and activity levels. Whether you prefer hiking through natural reserves, bird watching in serene wetlands, engaging in exciting watersports, or enjoying a round of golf or tennis, the island's natural beauty and recreational opportunities ensure a memorable outdoor experience for all.

8. Shopping and Souvenirs

- Unique Boutiques and Markets

Île de Ré offers a delightful shopping experience with its unique boutiques and vibrant markets:

Market Day: Each village and town on the island has its own market day, where you can explore a variety of stalls selling local produce, artisanal goods, and crafts. The most famous of these is the St. Martin de Ré market, which takes place every day in the summer months. Here, you'll find everything from fresh seafood and fruits to handmade jewelry and clothing.

Artisan Boutiques: Wander through the charming streets of Île de Ré's villages, and you'll come across numerous artisan boutiques. These shops offer a range of products, from handmade jewelry and ceramics to local artwork and clothing. Don't miss the chance to purchase one-of-a-kind pieces that capture the island's essence.

Culinary Delights: Visit local food markets to sample and purchase island specialties. Look for stalls selling freshly caught seafood, regional cheeses, artisanal jams, and the famous fleur de sel (flower of salt) harvested from the island's salt marshes.

- Traditional Island Products

When shopping for souvenirs on Île de Ré, consider these traditional island products:

Salt Products: Île de Ré's salt marshes produce some of the world's finest fleur de sel. You can buy this delicate sea salt as well as salted caramels, biscuits, and other salt-based products as unique island souvenirs.

Potatoes: The island is renowned for its early potatoes, known locally as "la pomme de terre de l'île de Ré." Purchase a bag of these flavorful potatoes to enjoy a taste of the island's agricultural heritage.

Oysters: Île de Ré is famous for its oysters, which are considered among the best in France. Buy a dozen or more from local oyster farmers or seafood markets to savor the island's culinary excellence.

Wine: While the island itself is not a wine-producing region, you can find a selection of wines from nearby areas in local wine shops. Ask for recommendations on wines that pair well with the island's seafood dishes.

- Where to Buy Handmade Crafts

If you're interested in purchasing handmade crafts as souvenirs or gifts, Île de Ré offers several options:

Artisan Markets: Keep an eye out for artisan markets and craft fairs that often take place during the summer season. These events feature local artists and craftsmen showcasing their handmade creations, including pottery, jewelry, textiles, and more.

Art Galleries: Many art galleries on the island display and sell the works of local and visiting artists. Whether you're looking for paintings, sculptures, or other forms of visual art, you'll find a diverse range of options.

Pottery Studios: Île de Ré has a thriving pottery scene. Visit pottery studios and workshops to admire and purchase unique ceramic pieces that reflect the island's maritime charm.

Handmade Soaps and Cosmetics: Look for boutiques and markets selling handmade soaps, cosmetics, and skincare products crafted from natural ingredients. These items make for thoughtful and fragrant souvenirs.

Tax-Free Shopping Tips

While shopping on Île de Ré, keep in mind these tips for tax-free shopping:

VAT Refund: If you're a non-European Union resident, you may be eligible for a Value Added Tax (VAT) refund on certain purchases made on the island. Look for participating stores displaying the "Tax-Free Shopping" sign and inquire about the VAT refund process.

Minimum Purchase: There's typically a minimum purchase requirement to qualify for a VAT refund. Ensure that your total purchases meet this threshold to be eligible for the refund.

Keep Receipts: Retain all your purchase receipts and ask for a Tax-Free Shopping Cheque (a form provided by the store) when making eligible purchases. You'll need these documents to claim your VAT refund at the airport or designated refund points.

Valid Passport: When claiming your VAT refund, have your passport and any necessary documents ready for verification.

Île de Ré's shopping scene provides ample opportunities to find unique souvenirs, local delicacies, and handmade crafts that capture the island's charm. Whether you're exploring markets, artisan boutiques, or art galleries, shopping here is not just about acquiring items but also about immersing yourself in the island's culture and traditions.

9. Dining and Nightlife

- Authentic Île de Ré Cuisine

Île de Ré offers a culinary journey that showcases the best of regional and local flavors. Embrace the island's authentic cuisine by indulging in:

Seafood Platters: Begin your culinary adventure with a seafood platter, a true highlight of Île de Ré's gastronomy. Savor freshly caught oysters, mussels, shrimp, and crab, often served with a zesty mignonette sauce and accompanied by crisp white wine.

Salt-Marsh Lamb: Taste the island's unique salt-marsh lamb, known for its tender, flavorful meat. It's typically prepared with fresh herbs and roasted to perfection.

Potatoes: Sample the island's renowned early potatoes, La pomme de terre de l'île de Ré. These small, waxy potatoes are a local delicacy, often served with a drizzle of olive oil and a sprinkle of fleur de sel.

Market Delights: Explore the island's vibrant markets and savor local products like artisanal cheeses, fresh produce, and pastries. Try traditional island dishes like galette charentaise, a savory buckwheat crepe filled with ham and cheese.

- ## Local Seafood Specialties

Île de Ré's seafood offerings are a highlight of its culinary scene:

Oysters: The island's oysters are renowned for their exceptional quality and flavor. Enjoy them fresh from oyster shacks, where you can watch oyster farmers shuck them before your eyes.

Mussels: Île de Ré's mussels are often prepared in a fragrant broth with white wine, garlic, and parsley. They're a delightful starter or main course.

Salt-Marsh Shrimp: These small, sweet shrimp are harvested from the island's salt marshes.

Try them in various seafood dishes or as a topping for salads and pastas.

Fish: Sample locally caught fish like sea bass, sea bream, and monkfish, prepared in various ways, from grilled to poached in a delicate sauce.

- Beachfront Dining and Romantic Eateries

Dining on Île de Ré is not just about the food; it's also about the enchanting settings:

Beachfront Cafes: Enjoy casual beachfront dining at cafes that line the coast. Sip a glass of chilled wine while gazing at the sunset over the Atlantic.

Quaint Village Restaurants: Explore the island's charming villages and discover quaint restaurants tucked away in cobblestone alleys. These romantic eateries offer intimate settings and a taste of local cuisine.

Harbor Views: Dine at restaurants overlooking picturesque harbors, where you can watch fishing boats come and go while you savor your meal.

Fine Dining: For a special evening, consider booking a table at one of the island's fine-dining establishments, where talented chefs create exquisite dishes that blend traditional and contemporary flavors.

- Nightclubs and Entertainment

While Île de Ré is primarily known for its tranquil atmosphere, you can still find some entertainment options for your evenings:

Live Music: Some beachfront bars and restaurants host live music performances, creating a laid-back and enjoyable atmosphere.

Beach Parties: During the summer months, a few beach clubs organize beach parties with DJs, cocktails, and dancing. It's a fun way to experience nightlife on the island.

Nightclubs in La Rochelle: If you're craving more nightlife options, consider taking a short ferry ride to La Rochelle on the mainland. This historic city boasts a vibrant nightlife scene, with nightclubs, bars, and live music venues.

Île de Ré's dining and nightlife scene offers a delightful blend of authenticity, coastal flavors, and romantic settings. Whether you're indulging in seafood platters, dining with a view of the beach, or enjoying live music by the sea, your evenings on the island will be as memorable as your days spent exploring its natural beauty.

10. Family-Friendly Activities

- Kid-Friendly Beaches and Playgrounds

Île de Ré is a fantastic destination for families with children, offering numerous kid-friendly beaches and playgrounds:

Le Bois-Plage-en-Ré Beach: This beach is ideal for families with young children due to its calm waters and shallow depths. The fine sandy shore provides a safe and enjoyable environment for building sandcastles and playing beach games.

La Couarde-sur-Mer Beach: Another family-friendly option, this beach boasts a wide stretch of sand and gentle waves. Children can enjoy swimming, and there are often beachside play areas to keep them entertained.

Playgrounds: Many villages and towns on the island have well-maintained playgrounds with swings, slides, and climbing structures. These provide a perfect opportunity for kids to burn off some energy and make new friends.

- Family-Friendly Attractions

Île de Ré offers a range of family-friendly attractions to explore:

Le Jardin de la Brande: This delightful garden in La Flotte features a variety of plants, ponds, and pathways. It's a tranquil place for families to stroll and enjoy nature. Look out for the resident ducks and geese.

La Maison du Magayant: Located in Ars-en-Ré, this interactive nature center is perfect for kids. It features exhibitions and activities that educate children about the island's unique environment, including salt marshes and dunes.

Phare des Baleines: Climb to the top of this iconic lighthouse on the island's western tip for panoramic views of the coastline. Kids will love the adventure of ascending the steps and learning about maritime history.

Les ânes de Ré: Treat your family to a memorable experience by taking a guided donkey ride around the island. It's a fun and unique way to explore the natural beauty of Île de Ré.

Le Labyrinthe en Ré: This family-friendly attraction in La Couarde-sur-Mer features a giant maze made of tall hedges. Kids can navigate through the labyrinth while adults can relax in the garden.

- Tips for Traveling with Children

When traveling with children on Île de Ré, consider these valuable tips to ensure a smooth and enjoyable experience:

Pack Essentials: Make sure to bring essential items for your children, including sunscreen, hats, swimsuits, and insect repellent. Also, carry any necessary medications, baby supplies, and comfort items.

Water Safety: Keep a close watch on children when they are near the water, even in calm areas. Consider using life jackets or floatation devices for added safety, especially if your children are not strong swimmers.

Plan Kid-Friendly Activities: Research family-friendly activities and attractions in advance to ensure you have options that cater to your children's interests and energy levels.

Rest and Snack Breaks: Children may need regular breaks for rest and snacks. Bring along snacks and water to keep them fueled and hydrated during your adventures.

Child-Friendly Accommodations: Choose accommodations that are suitable for families, such as those with family rooms or apartments. Check if they offer amenities like cribs, high chairs, and play areas.

Engage with Locals: Île de Ré residents are typically warm and welcoming. Encourage your children to interact with local children at playgrounds and parks, providing opportunities for cultural exchange and new friendships.

Île de Ré's family-friendly atmosphere, safe beaches, and engaging attractions make it an ideal destination for a memorable vacation with children. By planning ahead and considering your children's needs and interests, you can ensure that your family enjoys a fantastic and stress-free experience on this beautiful island.

11. Wellness and Relaxation

- Spas and Wellness Centers

While Île de Ré is known for its natural beauty and outdoor activities, it also offers opportunities for relaxation and rejuvenation at spas and wellness centers:

Thalassotherapy Spas: The island is home to several thalassotherapy centers, which utilize the healing properties of seawater, algae, and marine mud to promote well-being. Treat yourself to treatments such as seaweed wraps, hydrotherapy baths, and massages in a serene and coastal setting.

Spa Resorts: Many luxury resorts on the island have their own spa facilities, offering a range of treatments and therapies. Indulge in massages, facials, and body scrubs, and then unwind in saunas, steam rooms, and relaxation areas.

Wellness Retreats: Consider booking a wellness retreat that combines yoga, meditation, spa treatments, and healthy dining. These retreats provide a holistic approach to relaxation and rejuvenation, often set in tranquil natural surroundings.

- Yoga Retreats

Île de Ré's serene environment makes it an ideal location for yoga retreats and classes.

Here's how you can incorporate yoga into your wellness journey on the island:

Yoga Retreats: Several wellness centers and resorts on the island offer yoga retreats that cater to all levels, from beginners to advanced practitioners. Retreats often include daily yoga sessions, meditation, healthy meals, and time for relaxation and exploration.

Beach Yoga: Enjoy the tranquility of the island's beaches by participating in beach yoga classes. Practicing yoga on the sand with the sound of the ocean in the background is a rejuvenating experience.

Private Sessions: Some wellness centers and yoga instructors offer private sessions, allowing you to receive personalized guidance and tailored practices to meet your specific wellness goals.

Meditation and Mindfulness on the Island

Île de Ré's natural beauty and peaceful atmosphere create an ideal environment for meditation and mindfulness practices:

Beach Meditation: The island's serene beaches provide the perfect backdrop for meditation. Find a quiet spot by the shore, close your eyes, and focus on the soothing sounds of the waves and the gentle caress of the sea breeze.

Nature Walks: Explore the island's nature reserves and walking trails while practicing mindfulness. Pay attention to the sights, sounds, and sensations of the natural world around you to enhance your connection with the environment.

Meditation Workshops: Look for meditation workshops and classes offered by local instructors or wellness centers. These sessions can help you learn new techniques and deepen your mindfulness practice.

Wellness Retreats: As mentioned earlier, wellness retreats often incorporate meditation and mindfulness practices into their programs. Participating in a retreat is a great way to immerse yourself in these activities and experience their benefits.

Île de Ré's emphasis on natural beauty, tranquility, and holistic well-being makes it an excellent destination for those seeking relaxation and mindfulness. Whether you prefer spa treatments, yoga sessions, meditation on the beach, or a combination of these activities, the island provides the perfect setting to unwind and find inner peace.

12. Practical Tips and Safety

Health and Safety Information

Emergency Services: In case of emergencies, dial 112, the European emergency number, for police, medical assistance, or fire services. Île de Ré has a hospital in La Rochelle, and medical clinics and pharmacies are available on the island.

Health Insurance: Ensure you have comprehensive travel insurance that covers medical emergencies. European Health Insurance Cards (EHIC) may be valid, so check with your local health authorities before traveling.

Sun Safety: Protect yourself from the sun by wearing sunscreen, sunglasses, and a wide-brimmed hat. Dehydration and heatstroke are concerns during hot summer months, so stay hydrated and seek shade when needed.

Water Safety: While Île de Ré generally has calm waters, always be cautious when swimming, especially with children. Follow safety guidelines, adhere to beach flags and lifeguard instructions, and be aware of tides and currents.

COVID-19: Stay informed about the latest COVID-19 guidelines and restrictions in place during your visit. Follow local regulations, wear masks indoors if required, and maintain social distancing when necessary.

- Packing Essentials for Île de Ré

Beach Essentials: If you plan to spend time on the beach, pack swimwear, beach towels, sun hats, and beach chairs or mats. Water shoes can be useful for rocky shorelines.

Comfortable Clothing: Bring lightweight and breathable clothing for warm summer days. Layering is recommended for cooler evenings or occasional rain. Don't forget comfortable walking shoes for exploring the island.

Sun Protection: Sunscreen, sunglasses, and sun hats are crucial to protect yourself from the strong sun. Consider a small first-aid kit with basic supplies like adhesive bandages, antiseptic wipes, and pain relievers.

Reusable Water Bottle: Reduce plastic waste by carrying a reusable water bottle. The tap water on Île de Ré is safe to drink, so you can refill your bottle as needed.

Plug Adapters: The island uses Type E (French) electrical outlets. If your devices have a different plug type, bring a suitable adapter.

Cash and Cards: While there are ATMs and card payment options, it's advisable to carry some cash for small purchases, especially in rural areas.

- Emergency Contacts and Services

Emergency Services: Dial 112 for all emergencies, including police, medical, and fire services.

Police: In non-emergency situations, you can contact the local police station at 17.

Medical Services: In case of a medical emergency, contact the nearest medical clinic or hospital. For non-urgent medical needs, visit a pharmacy (pharmacie) on the island.

Lost or Stolen Items: Report lost or stolen items to the local police station and your embassy or consulate, if applicable. Keep a copy of your passport and important documents in a separate location from the originals.

Travel Insurance: Keep your travel insurance information readily available, including the policy number and contact details for assistance.

- Sustainable Travel Practices

Respect Nature: Île de Ré is home to a delicate ecosystem. Stay on designated paths, avoid disturbing wildlife, and dispose of waste properly. Follow the Leave No Trace principles to minimize your environmental impact.

Reduce Plastic Use: Bring a reusable shopping bag, water bottle, and cutlery to reduce single-use plastic consumption. Participate in beach cleanups if available.

Use Public Transportation: Explore the island using eco-friendly modes of transport like bicycles and public buses to reduce carbon emissions and traffic congestion.

Support Local Businesses: Choose locally-owned restaurants, shops, and accommodations to contribute to the island's economy and culture.

Conserve Water and Energy: Be mindful of water and energy use in accommodations. Turn off lights and appliances when not in use, and limit shower times to conserve resources.

By adhering to these practical tips and safety guidelines, you can enjoy a safe and sustainable visit to Île de Ré while making the most of its natural beauty and cultural offerings.

13. Day Trips and Excursions

- Exploring Nearby Islands

While Île de Ré itself is a stunning destination, you can enhance your experience by embarking on day trips to nearby islands, each offering its own unique charm:

Île d'Oléron: Known as the "Bright Island," Île d'Oléron is France's second-largest island and is famous for its beautiful beaches, oyster farming, and the impressive Château d'Oléron. You can reach Île d'Oléron via a bridge from the mainland.

Île d'Aix: This small and car-free island is a true hidden gem. Explore its quaint village, historic fortifications, and pristine beaches. Access Île d'Aix via a ferry from Fouras, on the mainland.

Fort Boyard: While you can't visit the fort itself, you can take boat tours that pass by this iconic structure. Learn about its history and watch as it looms on the horizon.

Réserve Naturelle Nationale du Marais d'Yves: Located on the mainland near Rochefort, this nature reserve is a haven for birdwatching and wildlife enthusiasts. Walk along the trails and boardwalks to observe the diverse ecosystem.

- Mainland Adventures

Venturing to the mainland offers a wealth of opportunities for exploration:

La Rochelle: Explore the historic port city of La Rochelle, located just a short bridge away from Île de Ré. Visit its vibrant Old Town, tour the maritime museums, and savor fresh seafood at the bustling market.

Rochefort: Discover the maritime history of Rochefort by visiting the Corderie Royale (Royal Rope Factory) and the Hermione, a meticulously crafted replica of the 18th-century frigate that took Lafayette to America.

Cognac: A day trip to the town of Cognac is a treat for spirits enthusiasts. Tour Cognac distilleries, learn about the production process, and sample some of the finest brandies in the world.

Puy du Fou: While a bit farther from Île de Ré, the Puy du Fou historical theme park offers a unique experience. Witness spectacular live performances that transport you through different periods of history.

- Wine Tasting in the Surrounding Region

Cognac: The Cognac region is famous for its eponymous brandy. Take a guided tour of Cognac houses and distilleries to learn about the production process and indulge in tastings of this exquisite spirit.

Vineyards: The surrounding region of Charente-Maritime is known for its wine production. Visit local vineyards and wineries to sample wines like Pineau des Charentes and Bordeaux varietals.

Île de Ré Wines: While on the island, don't miss the opportunity to taste its own wines, which include whites, rosés, and reds. Many local wineries offer tours and tastings.

- Organized Tours and Excursions

Consider joining organized tours and excursions to make the most of your day trips:

Boat Tours: Choose from a variety of boat tours, including cruises around the island, trips to nearby islands, and whale watching tours. These tours often provide informative guides and opportunities to spot marine life.

Bicycle Tours: Explore Île de Ré and the surrounding areas on two wheels with guided bicycle tours. These tours can take you to scenic spots and provide historical context about the region.

Food and Wine Tours: Join gastronomic tours that introduce you to the island's culinary delights or take you on a wine-tasting journey through the surrounding vineyards.

Historical and Cultural Tours: Guided tours can enhance your understanding of the region's history, architecture, and culture. Explore ancient forts, museums, and charming villages with knowledgeable guides.

Day trips and excursions from Île de Ré offer a chance to broaden your horizons and experience the diverse landscapes, culture, and history of the Charente-Maritime region. Whether you're interested in exploring nearby islands, immersing yourself in mainland adventures, savoring local wines, or participating in organized tours, these experiences will add depth to your visit.

14. Local Insights and Hidden Gems

- Off the Beaten Path Destinations

While Île de Ré has its popular attractions, exploring off the beaten path can lead to hidden gems and unique experiences:

Les Portes-en-Ré: This picturesque village at the island's western tip is a serene escape from the crowds. Wander through its narrow streets, admire the traditional whitewashed houses, and visit the church with its distinctive black-and-white bell tower.

Le Phare des Baleines: While the lighthouse itself is a well-known landmark, many visitors miss the nearby museum. It offers fascinating insights into the history of lighthouses and the island's maritime heritage.

Le Marais des Bris: This lesser-known salt marsh on the island's northern coast is a serene place for a nature walk. Explore its peaceful trails and boardwalks, and keep an eye out for birdlife and other wildlife.

- Locals' Favorite Spots

Discovering Île de Ré from a local perspective can lead to memorable experiences:

Les Grenettes Beach: While Plage de Rivedoux is popular, locals often head to Les Grenettes Beach for a quieter atmosphere. It's perfect for windsurfing and kiteboarding, and there's even a beachside bar for refreshments.

Le Marché de La Flotte: While the St. Martin de Ré market is bustling, the market in La Flotte is a favorite among locals. It's smaller but equally charming, with a focus on fresh produce, seafood, and artisanal products.

Village of Saint-Clément-des-Baleines: This village on the island's western coast has a relaxed vibe and is home to the Phare des Baleines. It's a favorite spot for sunset views and tranquil beach moments.

- Insider Tips for an Authentic Experience

To enjoy an authentic Île de Ré experience, consider these insider tips:

Sample Local Oysters: Visit oyster farms and shacks scattered across the island to taste fresh oysters right where they're harvested. It's a unique and delicious experience.

Attend a Village Festival: Keep an eye out for local festivals and events happening during your visit. These celebrations often feature traditional music, dancing, and culinary delights.

Explore the Salt Marshes: Take a guided tour of the salt marshes to gain insight into the island's salt production heritage and its ecological importance.

Savor a Bike Ride: Rent a bike and explore the island's extensive network of cycling paths.

It's a leisurely way to discover hidden corners and enjoy the natural beauty.

Embrace the Slow Pace: Île de Ré has a relaxed and unhurried atmosphere. Embrace the island's slow pace of life, savor long meals at local restaurants, and take time to unwind.

Connect with Locals: Strike up conversations with locals at markets, cafes, and shops. They can provide valuable insights and recommendations for authentic experiences.

By venturing off the beaten path, seeking out locals' favorite spots, and following insider tips, you'll uncover the hidden gems and authentic charm that make Île de Ré a truly special destination. These experiences will deepen your connection to the island's culture and natural beauty.

15. Conclusion

- Farewell to Île de Ré

As your time on Île de Ré comes to a close, you'll likely find it hard to bid farewell to this enchanting island. The tranquil beaches, charming villages, and rich cultural experiences will leave a lasting imprint on your heart. Before you leave, take a moment to savor the island's unique atmosphere one last time.

Memories to Cherish

Throughout your journey on Île de Ré, you've undoubtedly collected a treasure trove of memories to cherish. The sound of waves lapping against the shore, the taste of freshly shucked oysters, the warmth of the sun on your skin as you pedaled through picturesque villages—these moments will linger in your mind, serving as a reminder of the island's beauty and charm.

As you reflect on your time here, remember the laughter shared with loved ones, the exploration of hidden corners, and the connections made with friendly locals. These memories are the true souvenirs of your adventure.

Planning Your Next Adventure

While saying goodbye to Île de Ré may be bittersweet, the world is full of other captivating destinations waiting to be explored. As you return home or set off on your next journey, take the lessons and experiences from Île de Ré with you. Whether it's a newfound appreciation for the simple pleasures in life or a desire to seek out more hidden gems, your time on the island has likely left you with a sense of wanderlust.

As you plan your next adventure, whether it takes you to distant lands or brings you back to Île de Ré, remember that the world is a vast and wondrous place, rich in diversity and beauty. The spirit of exploration and the quest for new experiences will continue to enrich your life's journey.

In the end, Île de Ré is more than just a destination; it's a place that inspires a deeper connection with nature, culture, and the simple joys of life. It's a place where memories are made, and where the essence of relaxation and serenity permeates every moment. Until your next adventure, may the spirit of Île de Ré remain with you, guiding you toward new horizons and unforgettable experiences.

Printed in Great Britain
by Amazon